AF228587

XTREME SPEED

THE WORLD'S FASTEST MOTORCYCLES

A&D Xtreme
BOLD HI-LO NONFICTION
An imprint of Abdo Publishing
abdobooks.com

S.L. HAMILTON

TAKE IT TO THE XTREME!

GET READY FOR AN XTREME ADVENTURE!
THE PAGES OF THIS BOOK WILL TAKE YOU INTO THE THRILLING
WORLD OF THE FASTEST MOTORCYCLES ON EARTH.
WHEN YOU HAVE FINISHED READING THIS BOOK, TAKE THE
XTREME CHALLENGE ON PAGE 45 ABOUT WHAT YOU'VE LEARNED!

ABDOBOOKS.COM

Published by Abdo Publishing, a division of ABDO, PO Box 398166, Minneapolis, Minnesota 55439. Copyright © 2021 by Abdo Consulting Group, Inc. International copyrights reserved in all countries. No part of this book may be reproduced in any form without written permission from the publisher. A&D Xtreme™ is a trademark and logo of Abdo Publishing.

Printed in the United States of America, North Mankato, MN.

032020

092020

Editor: John Hamilton; Copy Editor: Bridget O'Brien

Graphic Design: Sue Hamilton; Imprint Template Design: Dorothy Toth

Cover Design: Victoria Bates

Cover Photo: Alamy

Interior Photos & Illustrations: Alamy-pgs 20-21, 32-33 & 36-37; American Flat Track-pg 25 (top); BMW-pgs 30-31; Aprilia-pgs 18-19; Coleman Power Sports-pgs 12-13; DirtBikes-pgs 24-25; Dukati-pgs 28-29; Harley-Davidson-pgs 25 (bottom) & 27 (bottom); iStock-pgs 8-11; Kawasaki-pgs 1, 33 (inset), 40 & 41; KTM-pgs 16-17; Lightning Motors-pgs 38-39; NHRA-pg 37 (inset); Nitrinos-pg 9 (inset top right); NLO-Moto-pg 9 (inset top middle); Shutterstock-pgs 4-5; Suzuki Motorcycles Philippines-pgs 14-15 & 34-35; TMC Dumont-pg 44; Typhoon-pg 9 (inset top left); Yamaha-pgs 22-23 & 26-27.

LIBRARY OF CONGRESS CONTROL NUMBER: 2019956099

PUBLISHER'S CATALOGING-IN-PUBLICATION DATA

Names: Hamilton, S.L., author.

Title: The world's fastest motorcycles / by S.L. Hamilton

Description: Minneapolis, Minnesota : Abdo Publishing, 2021 | Series: Xtreme speed | Includes online resources and index

Identifiers: ISBN 9781532193927 (lib. bdg.) | ISBN 9781098212704 (ebook)

Subjects: LCSH: Speed--Juvenile literature. | Motorcycles, Racing--Juvenile literature. | Motor vehicles--Juvenile literature. | Transportation--Juvenile literature.

Classification: DDC 629.046--dc23

TABLE OF CONTENTS

THE WORLD'S FASTEST MOTORCYCLES

Motorcycles give people thrills both on roads and off. With engines humming and the wind in their faces, motorcyclists love riding on some of the fastest machines on the planet.

Although motorcycles can go very fast, it's important to stay within speed limits. Some motorcycles may only be driven **off-road**. **Track-only** motorcycles are allowed on racetracks. Motorcycles that are **street legal** are safe to use on city roads at posted speeds.

A motorcyclist leans into a curve.

CHAPTER 2

MOTORCYCLE HISTORY

Motorcycles were first produced in 1894 in Germany. The top speeds were 25-28 mph (40-45 kph). Racing began near the turn of the century. In America in the 1910s and 1920s, **Harley-Davidson** and **Indian** motorcycles sped around dangerous tracks at more than 100 mph (161 kph).

Board track racing was fast and deadly. Motorcycles had no brakes and were raced on oily, steeply angled boards.

Motorcycle racing grew in popularity. Tracks became safer. By the 1950s, speeds had increased to 125 mph (201 kph). Motorcycles were built especially for track and **off-road** racing. Top speeds continued to go up.

CHAPTER 3

SAFETY GEAR

Safety helmets are designed to protect riders on streets and **off-road.** Many people show their personalities by the type of helmet they wear.

Spider-Man Off-Road Helmet

Predator Helmet

Cat Helmet

Helmets are made for safety, but can also be fun. From superheroes to movies to animals, there are many stylized helmets to choose from.

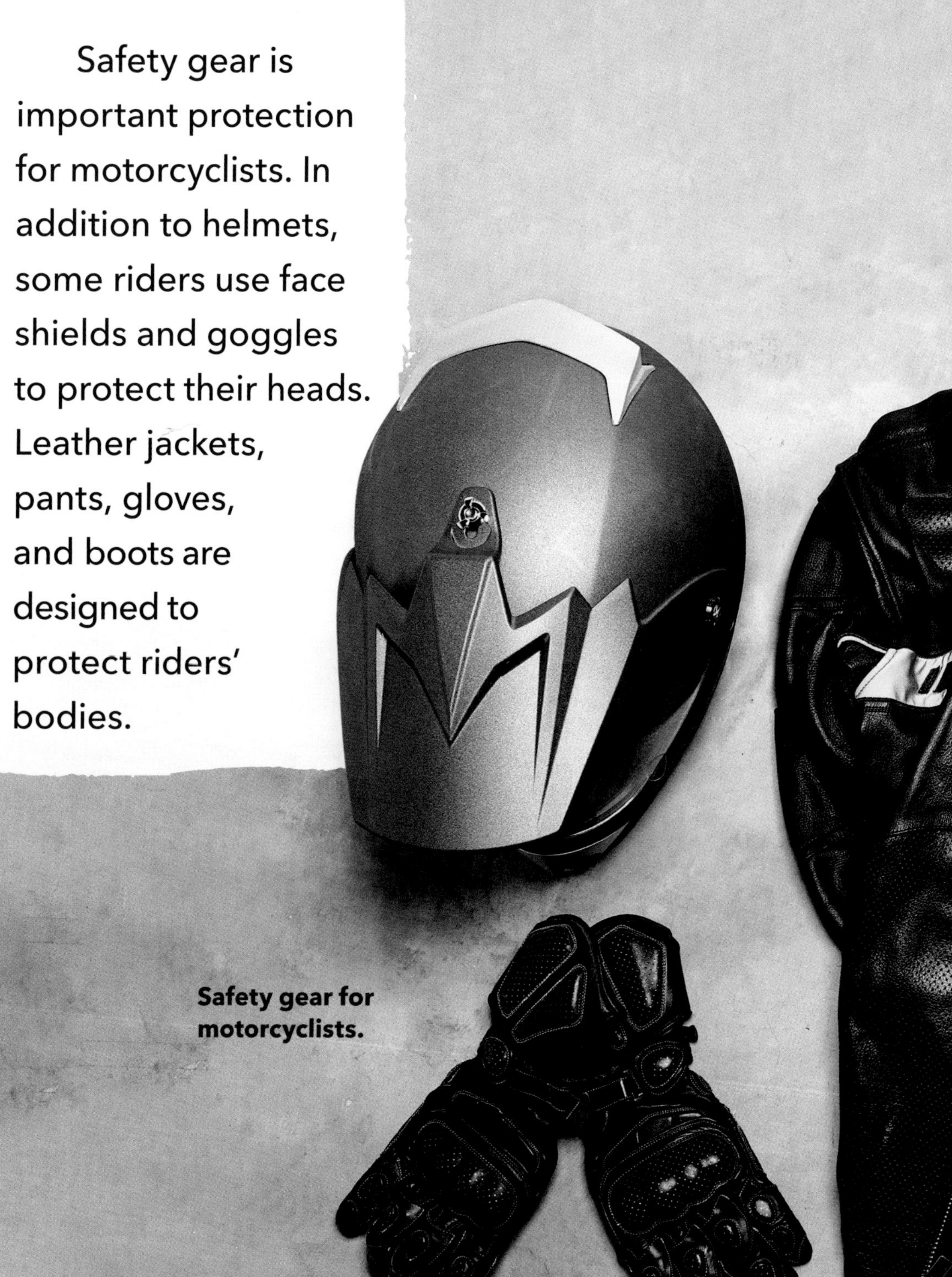

Safety gear is important protection for motorcyclists. In addition to helmets, some riders use face shields and goggles to protect their heads. Leather jackets, pants, gloves, and boots are designed to protect riders' bodies.

Safety gear for motorcyclists.

XTREME FACT

Indian Motorcycle's website states: "Always wear a helmet, eye protection, protective clothing, and obey the speed limit. Never ride under the influence of drugs or alcohol."

SPEED BEASTS

Minibikes are only about 20 inches (50 cm) tall. Kids as young as seven years old may drive these speedy bikes on trails.

Minibikes are not street legal because of their small size.

Coleman Powersports CT200U

Coleman Powersports CT100U and CT200U are currently the fastest minibikes. They reach a top speed of 25 mph (40 kph).

The fastest **underbone** motorcycle is the Suzuki Raider R150. It is nicknamed the "Underbone King." The sporty motorcycle's top speed is 91 mph (146 kph).

Suzuki Raider R150

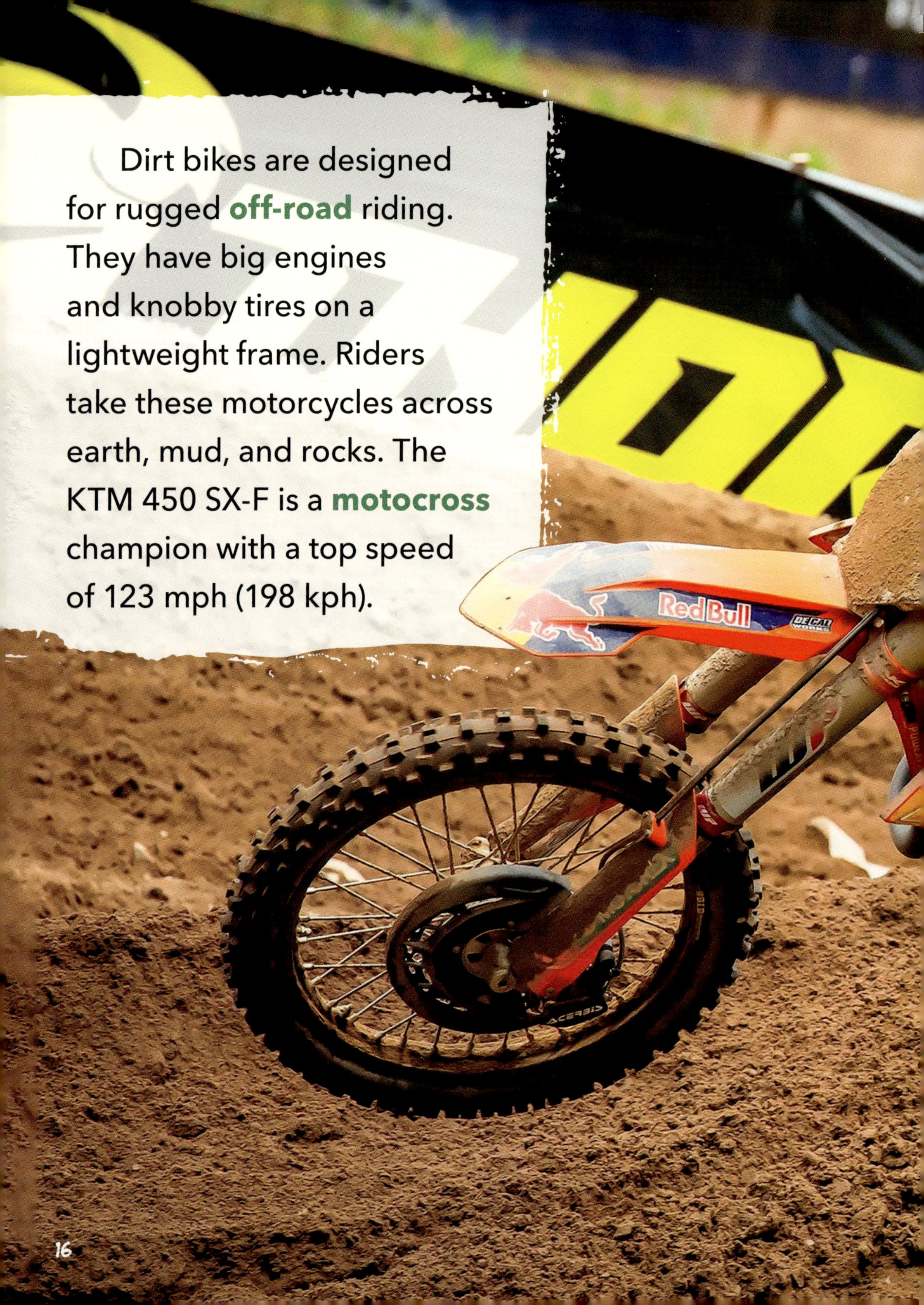

Dirt bikes are designed for rugged **off-road** riding. They have big engines and knobby tires on a lightweight frame. Riders take these motorcycles across earth, mud, and rocks. The KTM 450 SX-F is a **motocross** champion with a top speed of 123 mph (198 kph).

XTREME FACT

The fastest electric dirt bike is the Zero FX. It reaches a top speed of 85 mph (137 kph).

The Aprilia SRV 850 is a scooter with power. Many people call it a "super scooter." It can go up to 124 mph (200 kph).

XTREME FACT
According to Aprilia, the SRV 850's engine is uniquely designed to make it "the fastest and most powerful scooter ever manufactured anywhere in the world."

CHAPTER 5

SPEED MONSTERS

A chopper is a type of **cruiser** motorcycle. It has a long, low frame and stretched handlebars. Many are **custom-made** bikes. An average chopper has a top speed of about 140 mph (225 kph).

Choppers are often difficult to drive, but show the rider's style.

SPEED MONSTER
CHARACTERISTICS

TOP SPEED RANGE
140-160 mph
(225-257 kph)

SPEED MONSTER TYPES
Chopper, Standard, Flat
Track, Cruiser, Enduro

Standard motorcycles are often seen on city streets. Riders sit upright and are more visible in traffic. Some people think of them as "beginner" motorcycles, but standards can go fast! The Yamaha MT-09 has a top speed of 140 mph (225 kph).

XTREME FACT

Standards are also called "naked bikes" because they have limited bodywork.

Motorcycle flat track racing began in the United States in the early 1900s. **Harley-Davidson** and **Indian** motorcycles were the main vehicles used in the sport, and continue to be raced today.

The top speed of an Indian Scout FTR750 and Harley-Davidson XG750R is 140 mph (225 kph) on straightaways and 90 mph (145 kph) on curves. Racers are often only inches from each other.

Briar Bauman races an Indian Scout FTR750.

Dalton Gauthier races a Harley-Davidson XG750R.

XTREME FACT

Almost all flat track races are photo finishes. The riders cross the finish line within a second of each other.

Cruisers are designed for riding in style. The fastest power cruiser is the Yamaha Star VMAX. Its top speed is 150 mph (241 kph). It can go from 0-60 mph (0-97 kph) in 2.5 seconds.

Yamaha Star VMAX

XTREME FACT

Harley-Davidson has been the main producer of cruisers for decades. The Harley-Davidson V-Rods are some of the fastest cruisers in the world.

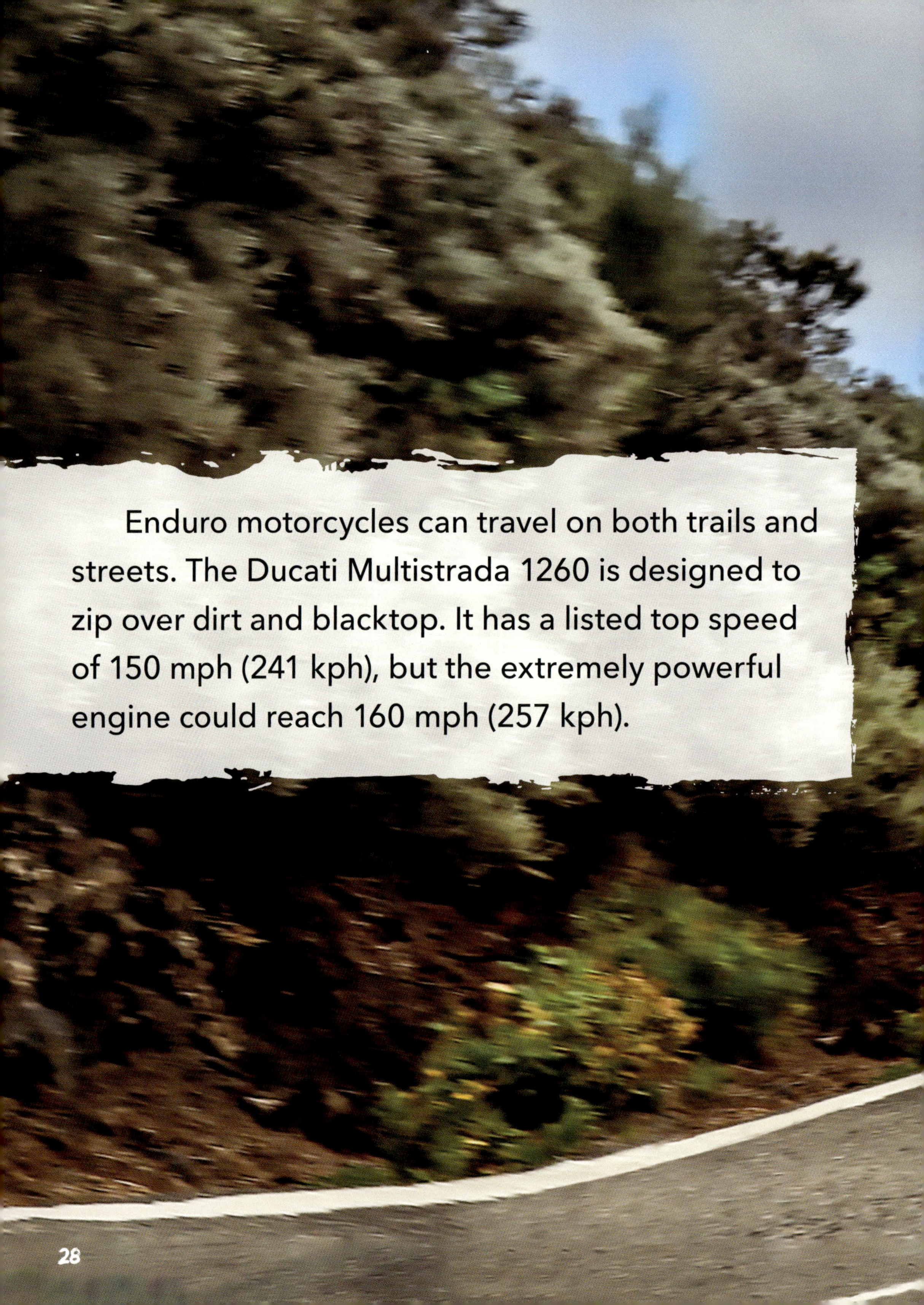

Enduro motorcycles can travel on both trails and streets. The Ducati Multistrada 1260 is designed to zip over dirt and blacktop. It has a listed top speed of 150 mph (241 kph), but the extremely powerful engine could reach 160 mph (257 kph).

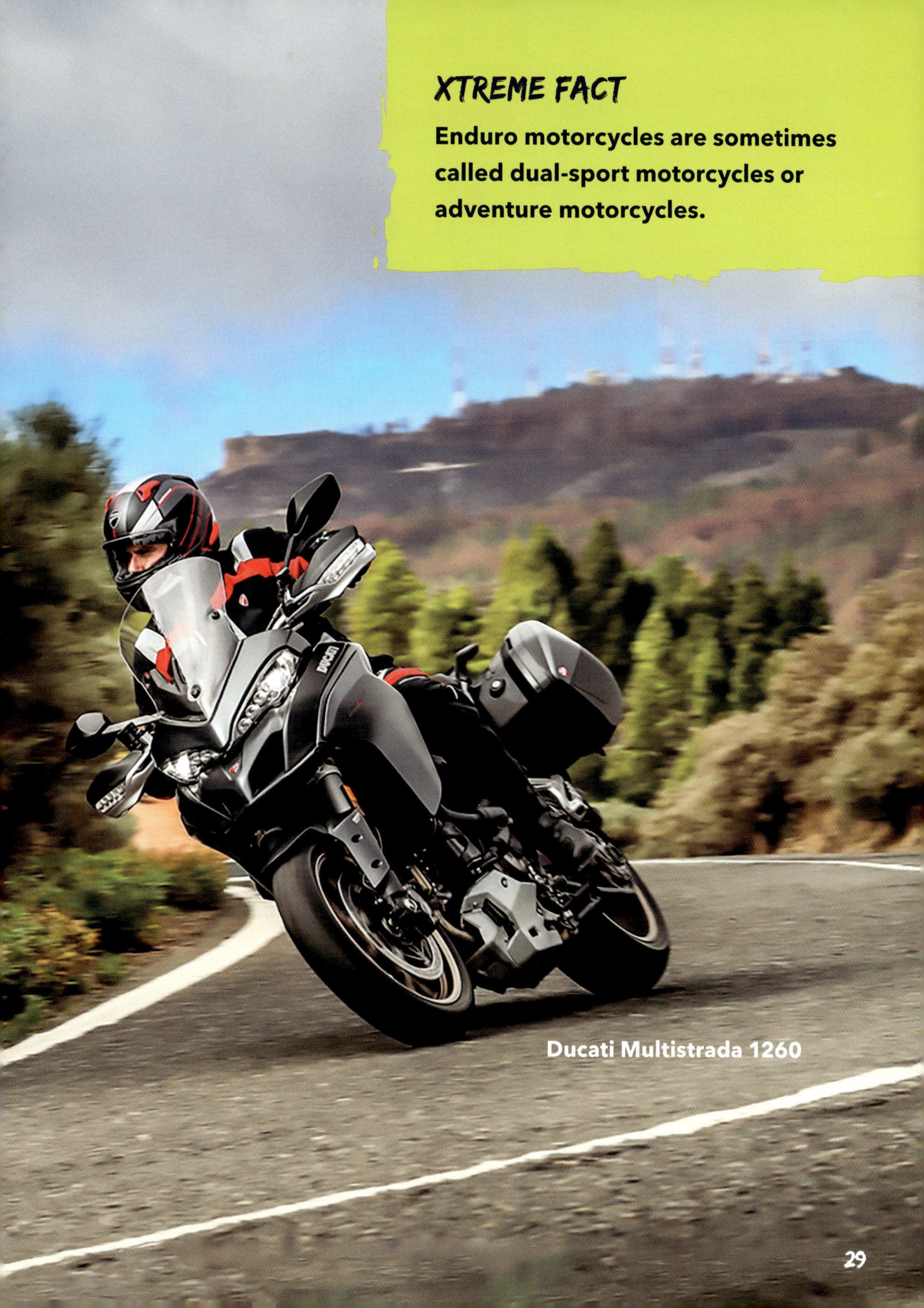

XTREME FACT

Enduro motorcycles are sometimes called dual-sport motorcycles or adventure motorcycles.

Ducati Multistrada 1260

CHAPTER 6

SPEED DEMONS

Sport bikes are known for their high performance. The fastest sport bike is the BMW S 1000 RR. It has a top speed of 190 mph (306 kph).

BMW
S 1000 RR

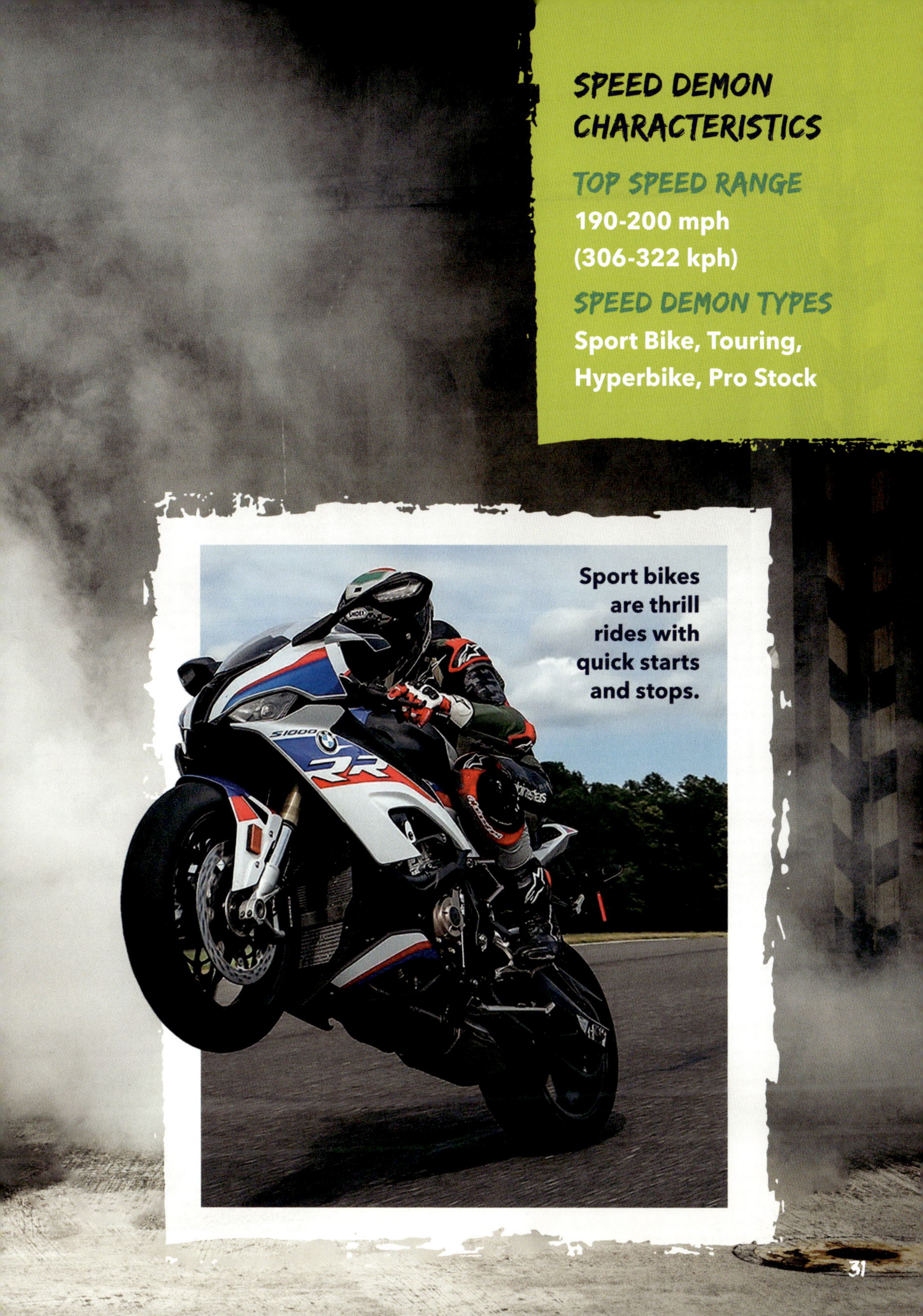

SPEED DEMON CHARACTERISTICS

TOP SPEED RANGE
190-200 mph
(306-322 kph)

SPEED DEMON TYPES
Sport Bike, Touring,
Hyperbike, Pro Stock

Sport bikes
are thrill
rides with
quick starts
and stops.

Touring bikes are made for
traveling long distances in comfort.
Honda created the fastest touring bike
with the CBR1100XX Super Blackbird.
Its top speed is 190 mph (306 kph).

XTREME FACT

The Kawasaki Ninja ZX-11 was the
top speed touring bike for eleven
years. It reached 176 mph (283 kph).

The Honda CBR1100XX
Super Blackbird was made
from 1996-2007.

Many Suzuki Hayabusa hyperbikes have speed limiters that keep them from reaching their dangerously high top speeds.

The Suzuki Hayabusa **hyperbike** was first introduced in 1999. Its top speed was 194 mph (312 kph). This caused so much concern about rider safety that Suzuki agreed to never create a faster **production motorcycle**.

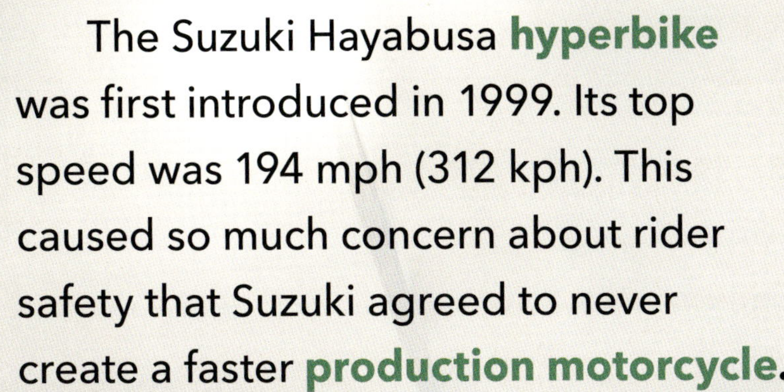

XTREME FACT

Hayabusa is the Japanese word for "peregrine falcon," the fastest bird on Earth.

Pro stock motorcycle drag racing is a seven-second rush. Riders on **custom-made** pro stock motorcycles compete against each other. They hurtle down a quarter-mile (0.4-km) track at a top speed of 200 mph (322 kph).

XTREME FACT

Hector Arana Jr. became the first pro stock motorcycle rider to break the 200 mph (322 kph) mark on March 16, 2018. His speed was 200.23 mph (322.24 kph).

CHAPTER 7

SPEED FREAKS

The Lightning LS-218 can go from 0-100 mph (0-161 kph) in 5.5 seconds. This powerful bike holds the current electric **production motorcycle** speed record of 218 mph (351 kph).

Lightning
LS-218

SPEED FREAK CHARACTERISTICS

TOP SPEED RANGE

218-350 mph
(351-563 kph)

SPEED FREAK TYPES

Electric, Superbike, Dodge Tomahawk

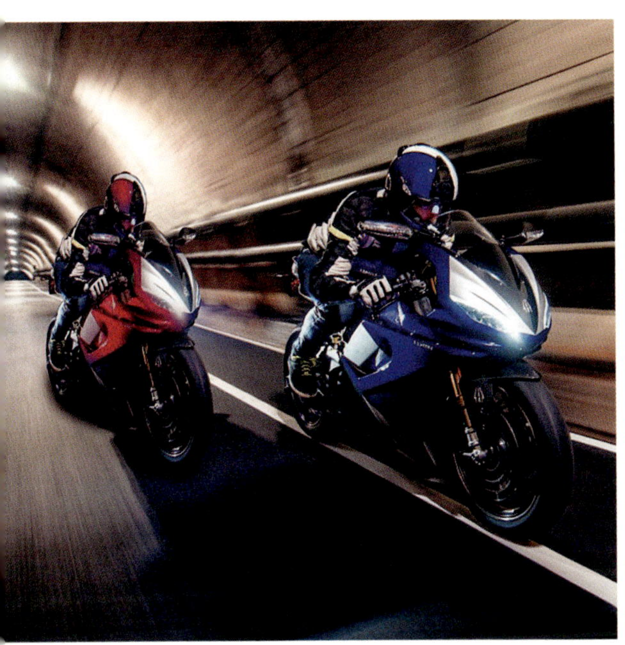

The Lightning LS-218 electric superbike can travel for 100 miles (161 km) at highway speeds before needing to recharge.

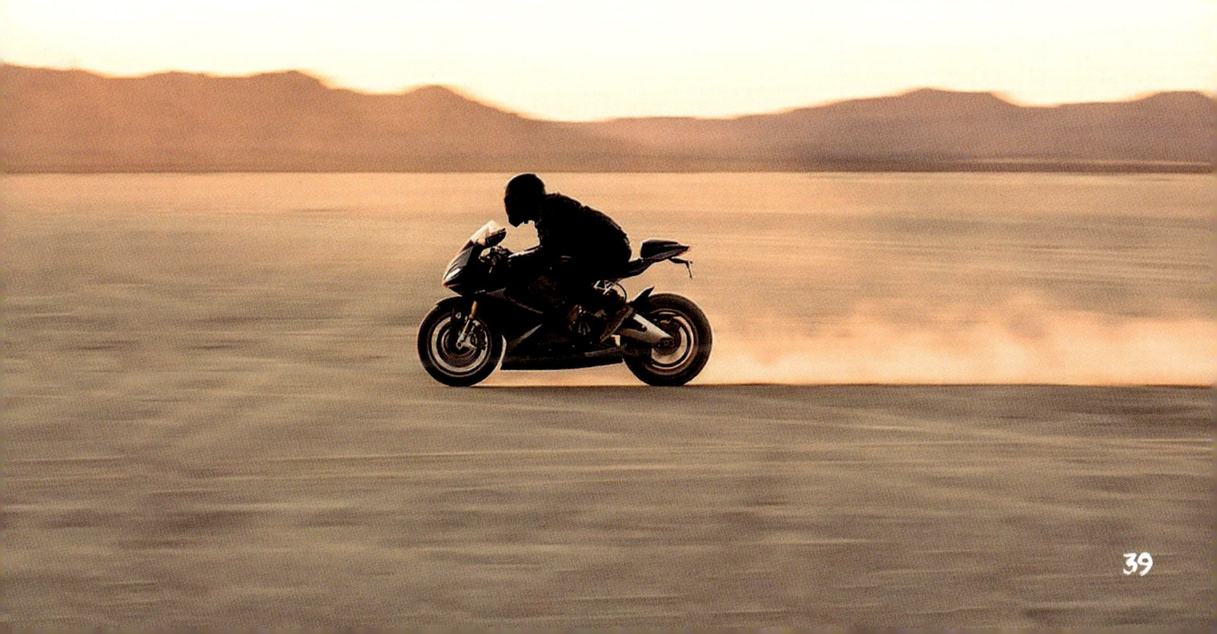

The fastest production superbike is the Kawasaki Ninja H2R. Its top speed is 249 mph (401 kph). This motorcycle is only driven on a racetrack.

XTREME FACT
The Kawasaki Ninja H2R has 50 percent more power than the fastest street-legal motorcycle.

The Dodge Tomahawk V10 is currently the fastest motorcycle ever made. It can go from 0-60 mph (0-97 kph) in just 1.5 seconds. The Tomahawk has a 10-cylinder engine clocked at a speed of 350 mph (563 kph). However, it has been estimated to have a top speed of 420 mph (676 kph). At that speed, the driver would likely be lifted off the vehicle!

XTREME FACT
The Tomahawk V10's top speed is about half as fast as the speed of sound!

CHAPTER 8

FUTURE CONCEPTS

Concept motorcycles are designs of the future. Hubless wheels, a hovercraft engine, radar alert systems, and automatic balancing are already being developed. Today's futuristic ideas may make motorcycles cooler, safer, and faster.

Formula 1 racer Tarso Marques has designed and built a concept motorcycle with hubless wheels and an aircraft engine.

XTREME CHALLENGE

**TAKE THE QUIZ BELOW AND
PUT WHAT YOU'VE LEARNED TO THE TEST!**

1) What is the youngest age a person can drive a motorcycle? What type of motorcycle can the youngest rider drive?

2) What is the difference between a "street legal" and an "off-road" motorcycle?

3) Is there a motorcycle that can travel at about half the speed of sound? If so, which one?

4) What safety gear is used by motorcyclists? Are there other items being developed that might help protect a rider in the future?

5) What are some new ideas being developed for concept motorcycles? Can you think of other ideas that engineers might want to work on?

GLOSSARY

concept motorcycle – An experimental motorcycle designed with new or unique features.

cruiser – A type of motorcycle where the rider usually sits in a laid-back posture with arms and feet forward.

custom-made – To create a one-of-a-kind type of vehicle, such as a motorcycle. This may include using unique parts, colors, and designs.

Harley-Davidson – An American motorcycle company that began operations in Milwaukee, Wisconsin, in 1903. Founders included William S. Harley and brothers Arthur, Walter, and William Davidson. The company is mostly known for its cruiser motorcycles.

hyperbike – A very high-performing, top-speed motorcycle.

Indian Motorcycles – An American company that began producing motorcycles in 1901. It was founded by bicycle racer George M. Hendee, who hired engineer Oscar Hedstrom to build gasoline-powered bikes.

motocross – A type of motorcycle race that is held on an outdoor, off-road track. Tracks range in length from 0.5 to 2 miles (0.8 to 3.2 km) and often include challenging jumps.

off-road – Driving on a trail, not on a paved street or road.

production motorcycle – Motorcycles made to sell to the general public.

street legal – Motorcycles equipped with lights, signals, and safety equipment that allow them to be ridden on a city's paved roads.

track only – Motorcycles designed to be raced on a track. Track-only motorcycles are often too powerful and fast to be ridden on city streets.

underbone – A class of small motorcycles built around a single tube frame (the "underbone") that supports the bike.

ONLINE RESOURCES

To learn more about the world's fastest motorcycles, please visit **abdobooklinks.com** or scan this QR code. These links are routinely monitored and updated to provide the most current information available.

INDEX